DATE DUE

DEMCO 128-8155

THE SCIENCE BEHIND

Plants

Rachel Lynette

Chicago, Illinois

www.capstonepub.com
Visit our website to find out
more information about
Heinemann-Raintree books.

To order:

☎ Phone 888-454-2279

🖥 Visit www.capstonepub.com
to browse our catalog and order online.

Edited by Megan Cotugno and Laura Knowles
Designed by Richard Parker
Picture research by Mica Brancic
Original Illustrations © Capstone Global Library
    Ltd 2012
Illustrations by Oxford Designers & Illustrators

Originated by Capstone Global Library Ltd
Printed and bound in China by Leo Paper
    Products Ltd

15 14 13 12 11
10 9 8 7 6 5 4 3 2 1

**Library of Congress Cataloging-in-Publication
Data**
Lynette, Rachel.
  Plants / Rachel Lynette.—1st ed.
    p. cm.—(The science behind)
  Includes bibliographical references and index.
  ISBN 978-1-4109-4484-9 (hc)—ISBN 978-1-4109-
4495-5 (pb) 1. Plants—Juvenile literature. I. Title.
II. Series: Science behind.

QK49.L96 2012
580—dc22   2011014587

Acknowledgments
We would like to thank the following for
permission to reproduce photographs: Getty
Images p. **7** (National Geographic/Bill Hatcher);
Science Photo Library p. **16** (John Durham);
Shutterstock pp. **5** (© Jose Ignacio Soto),
6 (© Slowfish), **9** (© Eva Madrazo), **10** (© Kasia),
11 (© Sherri R. Camp), **12** (© Szasz-Fabian Ilka
Erika), **18** (© irin-k), **20** (© Magone), **21** (© Selyutina
Olga), **22** (© Zurijeta), **23** (© Martin Fowler), **24**
(© Goodluz), **25** (© Drozdowski).

Cover photograph of a dandelion flower
reproduced with permission of Steve Mead.

We would like to thank David Crowther and Nancy
Harris for their invaluable help in the preparation
of this book.

Every effort has been made to contact copyright
holders of any material reproduced in this book.
Any omissions will be rectified in subsequent
printings if notice is given to the publisher.

Disclaimer
All the Internet addresses (URLs) given in this book
were valid at the time of going to press. However,
due to the dynamic nature of the Internet, some
addresses may have changed, or sites may have
changed or ceased to exist since publication. While
the author and publisher regret any inconvenience
this may cause readers, no responsibility for any
such changes can be accepted by either the author
or the publisher.

Contents

Look for these boxes:

Stay safe
These boxes tell you how to keep yourself and your friends safe from harm.

In your day
These boxes show you how science is a part of your daily life.

Measure up!
These boxes give you some fun facts and figures to think about.

Some words appear in bold, **like this**. You can find out what they mean by looking at the green bar at the bottom of the page or in the glossary.

Plants Are All Around Us

Look outside your window. What plants do you see? Are there tall trees? Are there leafy bushes? Are there beautiful flowers? There are many different kinds of plant, and they are everywhere! Some plants grow all by themselves, while others are planted by people.

We need plants

We need plants. Plants give us food. Fruits, nuts, and vegetables are all plants. Grains such as wheat and barley are plants, too. How many different plants have you eaten today? We use plants to build things such as houses and furniture. Plants also release **oxygen** into the air. People need oxygen to live. Animals need plants, too. Just like people, animals use plants for food, shelter, and oxygen.

In your day
Look around the room you are in now. How many things can you see that are made from paper or wood? Paper and wood are both made from plants and trees!

oxygen gas in the air

Plants need sunlight
to live.

Trees are the
largest plants.

Most flowers bloom in the
spring or summer.

Plants have leaves.

What Is a Plant?

A plant is alive. It grows just like you do. However, plants cannot move around like you can. Plants are **rooted**, or firmly planted, into the ground. Most plants grow in soil. Some plants can grow in sand or in areas that are very rocky. Some kinds of plants grow in the water. Water plants grow in lakes, ponds, and rivers. They also grow in salty water.

Water lilies have big leaves that float on the surface of the water.

rooted   firmly planted in the ground

6

Plants do not need to eat food to live like you do. They make their own food from water, air, **minerals,** and sunlight. Minerals are nutrients that plants get from the soil. They help them to grow. Plants are called **producers** because they make, or produce, their own food.

Stay safe

Some plants are harmful to people and to animals. Never eat berries or any other part of a plant that you find in the woods unless an adult has told you it is safe!

Some plants are very big, like this giant redwood tree.

Plant Parts

People have some of the same parts as each other, such as arms, ears, and toes. In the same way, plants also have some of the same parts as each other. Each part of a plant helps it to live and grow.

Roots

All plants have roots. Roots are the part of the plant that is underground. The roots keep the plant from falling over. They also **absorb**, or soak up, water and **minerals** from the soil to help the plant grow.

flower

leaves

stem

roots

absorb   soak up

Stems

The stem supports the plant. It helps the leaves to reach the sunlight. The stem also carries water and minerals from the roots into the rest of the plant. Most flowers have thin stems that are soft yet stiff. The trunk of a tree is a large, hard stem.

In your day

You have probably eaten roots many times. Whenever you eat a carrot or a sweet potato, you are eating the root part of a plant!

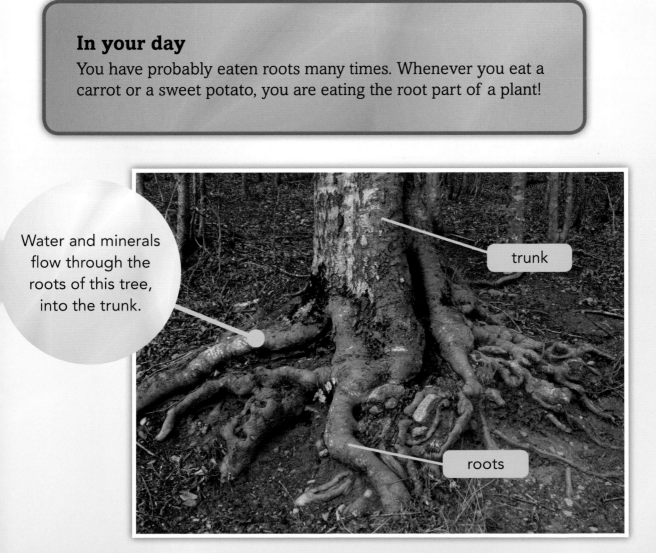

Water and minerals flow through the roots of this tree, into the trunk.

trunk

roots

Leaves

Leaves grow at the ends of stems. The leaves of a plant absorb sunlight. Many plants lose their leaves in the fall, when the weather turns cold. They will grow new leaves in the springtime, when there is more sunshine.

In some areas, flowers and other small plants start to grow their leaves a few weeks before trees do. That way their leaves can get some sunlight before the larger tree leaves block it out.

Look at a leaf up close. What do you see?

Flowers and fruit

Some plants, such as roses and daisies, also have flowers. Flowers grow from knob-like growths called **buds**. Flowers only bloom for part of the year, in the spring or summer. Some plants, such as apple trees, have small flowers, or blossoms. Fruit grows out of the blossoms. Fruit trees, berry bushes, and grape vines all have fruit that grows from blossoms.

These grapes grew from blossoms.

Measure up

Leaves come in different sizes. Use a ruler to find the smallest leaf that you can. What kind of plant did it come from? Then find the largest. What kind of plant did it come from?

bud   knob-like growth on a plant that grows into a flower or a leaf

It Starts with a Seed

A seed is a small part of a plant that can grow into a new plant. There are many different kinds of seeds. Beans, walnuts, and apple seeds are all seeds.

Seeds can come in different shapes and sizes. A poppy seed is so small that it can fit on the head of a pin. One of the largest seeds is a coconut.

These seeds are being planted in the soil.

Measure up

How many different seeds can you find? Look in your kitchen. Look outside. Make a list to count how many different kinds of seeds you find.

seed coat   hard outside part of a seed

Parts of a seed

All seeds have three main parts. The **seed coat** is on the outside. It is hard and protects the inside of the seed. The **embryo** is sometimes called the baby. It is the part that will grow into a plant. The rest of the seed is the **endosperm**. The endosperm is the food that the plant will need to grow.

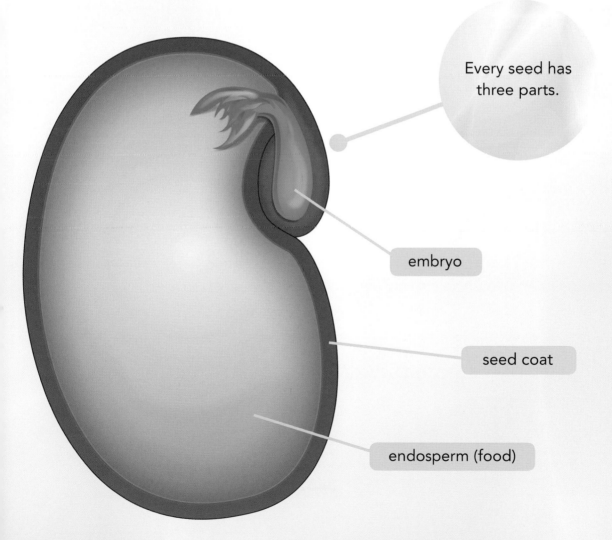

Every seed has three parts.

embryo

seed coat

endosperm (food)

embryo   baby plant inside a seed
endosperm food inside a seed

A sprouting seed

A seed needs heat and water to sprout, or **germinate**. The seed will wait until the soil is warm enough before it begins to grow.

First, water softens the seed coat. Then, a tiny root pushes through the seed coat down into the soil. Next, a tiny stem grows up toward the Sun. When the stem has pushed its way through the soil, leaves begin to grow. The leaves collect sunlight. Now the sprouting seed is called a **seedling**.

In your day

The kinds of sprouts you eat are actually seeds that are just beginning to grow. But do not worry—they will not continue to grow inside your stomach!

Most seeds never get to grow into plants. Some seeds get eaten by animals. Some do not find good soil to grow in or do not get enough water. Most plants produce a lot of seeds, so that at least some of them will grow into plants.

germinate   sprout and begin to grow
seedling   newly sprouted plant

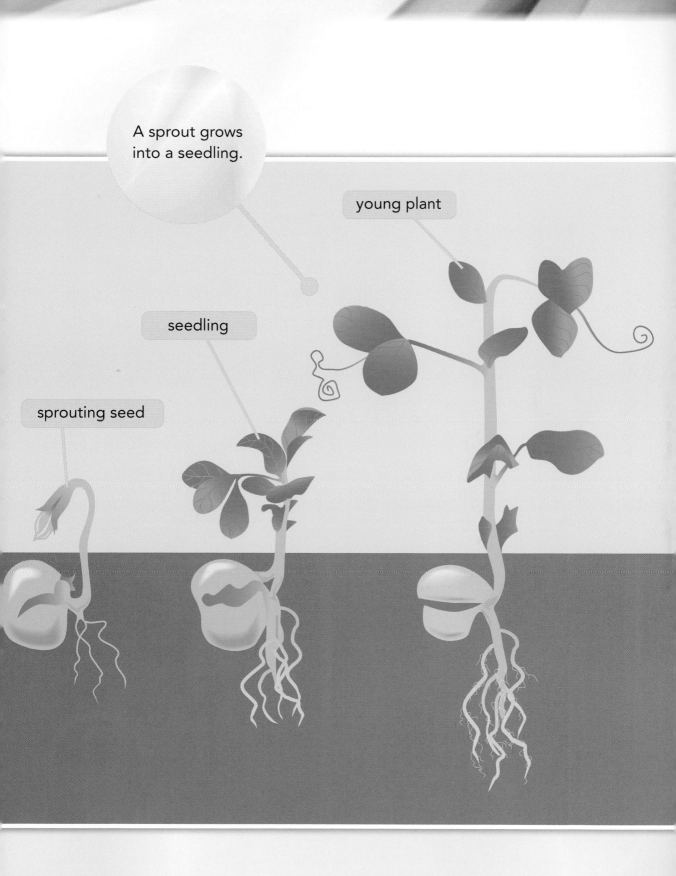

Growing Plants

All plants need five things to live. They need water, **minerals**, space, air, and sunlight.

Water

Cells are the building blocks of life. A plant is made from millions of tiny cells. The cells are filled with water. If the cells dry up, the plant will **wilt**, or droop, and die.

Minerals

Plants need minerals to grow. Plants use their roots to get minerals from the soil. The minerals must be mixed with water in order for the roots to **absorb** them.

These plant cells are so small you cannot see them without a microscope.

cell   building block of all living things
wilt   droop

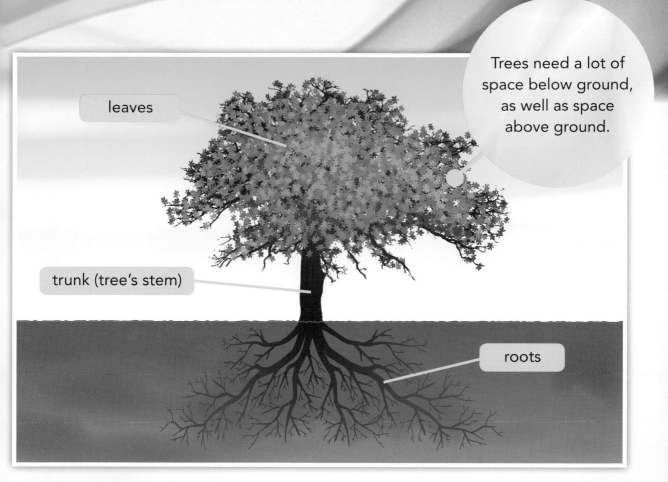

leaves

trunk (tree's stem)

roots

Trees need a lot of space below ground, as well as space above ground.

Space

Plants need room to grow above ground. If there are too many plants in one area, they will all have trouble finding enough room to grow. Plants also need room for their roots to grow below ground. Most plants cannot grow in areas with a lot of rocks or concrete.

In your day

Have you ever done any weeding in a garden? Most people do not like weeds because they take away space from other plants, making it harder for them to grow.

Sunlight and air

Plants do not eat food like people. They make their own food using water, air, and **energy** from the Sun. This process is called **photosynthesis**.

First, the leaves of the plant collect sunlight. They also collect a **gas** in the air called **carbon dioxide**. Then, the sunlight mixes with the carbon dioxide and water from the soil to create sugar. The plant uses the sugar for energy. The energy keeps the plant alive and growing. The process of photosynthesis also releases **oxygen** back into the air.

Plants need water, air, and sunlight to live.

Measure up

What do you think happens to a plant if it does not get any sunlight? Put a bucket over a weed or some other small outside plant. Check the plant every day. Did it get bigger or smaller? Did the color of the plant change?

energy   power
photosynthesis   process by which plants make their own food

This diagram shows how a plant uses photosynthesis to make its own food.

oxygen

sunlight

carbon dioxide

water

Staying Alive

It is not easy being a plant. Plants have many enemies, and they cannot run away like most animals. Many plants have developed ways to stay safe.

Animal enemies

Many plants get eaten by animals. Some plants, such as nettles, stay safe by having stinging leaves. Other plants, such as roses, have thorns. Some plants have **poisonous** berries. Others, like poison ivy, are covered with poisonous oil.

Goats and other grazing animals can eat a lot of plants every day.

poisonous   something that can cause pain or death

Plants that grow where it is very hot may have very long roots to find water. Most plants can store water in their leaves, roots, and stems.

Do not touch stinging nettles!

Stay safe

If you are walking in the woods, you may see poison ivy or stinging nettles. Be sure not to touch them! You could get a painful rash.

Making More Plants

Most plants make more plants by making seeds. A seed must leave the plant it came from in order to grow into a new plant. There are many ways that a seed can find a place to grow.

When you blow a dandelion, you are helping the seeds find a place to grow.

Traveling seeds

Some seeds travel on the wind. The seeds of maple trees have wings that make them spin like little helicopters. Dandelion seeds have tiny parachutes to help them catch a passing breeze.

Some seeds travel by water. A coconut that falls off a tree on the beach and rolls into the water can be carried to another island.

Animals can also carry seeds. Some seeds stick to an animal's fur. Other seeds grow inside fruit. When the fruit gets eaten by an animal, the seeds are carried inside the animal and released in the animal's droppings.

Sycamore seeds twirl like tiny helicopters as they are carried on the wind to new growing places.

In your day

Have you ever gotten **burrs** (tiny prickly balls) stuck on your clothes when you have been playing in a field or in the woods? Those burrs have seeds inside them. They travel by sticking to animals and people!

burr   prickly part of some plants that contains a seed

We Need Plants!

Plants are an important part of our world. We need plants to live. Plants give us **oxygen** so that we can breathe. Plants give us food to eat. We use trees to build houses and furniture. You are using plants right now because this book is made from paper—and paper comes from trees! Some plants can even give us medicine. Animals need plants, too. Many animals eat plants or make their homes in plants.

We can plant our own fruit, vegetable, and herb plants in our garden.

We need to take care of our world so that plants will have what they need to live. Plants need clean air and water. Plants need space to grow. Most plants need good soil that is full of **minerals**. What can you do to help plants live?

This person is washing away harmful pesticides.

Stay safe

Sometimes people try to keep plants safe by spraying them with **pesticides** to kill insect pests. Pesticides are not healthy for people. Always wash fruits and vegetables before you eat them!

pesticide   poison that is used to kill insects and other pests

25

Try It Yourself

Growing bean plants

Growing bean plants is a fun way to see how plants grow.

What you need

- bean seeds
- roll of paper towels
- jug of water
- plastic food bag
- small flowerpots
- potting soil

What to do

1. Start by choosing six to eight bean seeds.
2. Fold a paper towel into quarters. Then put enough water on it to make it damp.
3. Place the beans on top of the paper towel.
4. Fold a second piece of paper towel into quarters. Put enough water on it to make it damp.
5. Cover the first piece of paper towel with the beans on it with the second paper towel.
6. Carefully put the towels and the beans into a plastic food bag.

7. Check your bean seeds every day and add water if the towels start to dry out.
8. Make a drawing of one of your seeds as it sprouts.
9. When your seeds have sprouted, you can plant them in small pots full of potting soil. Put your pots in a sunny place and make sure they have enough water.
10. Every few days, use a ruler to measure one of your plants and record how much it has grown. You may also want to draw your plant as it grows. Remember to date your measurements and pictures. You may even want to make a chart to record your information.

Bean plant growth	
Date	Height
June 5, 2012	1 inch
June 8, 2012	2 inches

Glossary

absorb soak up

bud knob-like growth on a plant that grows into a flower or a leaf

burr prickly part of some plants that contains a seed

carbon dioxide gas in the air

cell building block of all living things

embryo baby plant inside a seed

endosperm food inside a seed

energy power

gas vapor that is neither a liquid nor a solid

germinate sprout and begin to grow

mineral material found in soil that helps plants to grow

oxygen gas in the air

pesticide poison that is used to kill insects and other pests

photosynthesis process by which plants make their own food

poisonous something that can cause pain or death

producer living thing that makes its own food

rooted firmly planted in the ground

seed coat hard outside part of a seed

seedling newly sprouted plant

wilt droop

Find Out More

Use these resources to find more fun and useful information about the science behind plants.

Books

Cook, Trevor. *Experiments with Plants and Other Living Things* (*Science Lab*). New York: PowerKids, 2009.

Llewellyn, Claire. *The Life of Plants* (*Understanding Plants*). North Mankato, Minn.: Smart Apple Media, 2008.

Malam, John. *Grow Your Own Butterfly Farm* (*Grow It Yourself!*). Chicago: Heinemann Library, 2012.

Malam, John. *Grow Your Own Snack* (*Grow It Yourself!*). Chicago: Heinemann Library, 2012.

Morgan, Sally. *The Plant Cycle* (*Nature's Cycles*). New York: Rosen/PowerKids, 2009.

Taylor-Butler, Christine. *Experiments with Plants* (*My Science Investigations*). Chicago: Heinemann Library, 2012.

Websites

www.biology4kids.com/files/plants_main.html
Learn all about plants at this website, which includes slideshows and quizzes.

www.blueplanetbiomes.org/plants.htm
Find information about how plants developed on Earth and what people use them for at this website.

http://kids.nationalgeographic.com/kids/activities/crafts/miniature-garden/
Find out how to grow your own miniature garden!

www.discovertheforest.org
Find out more about the Discover the Forest program, which encourages young people to get out into nature to experience plants and nature up close.

Index